THE
DIFFICULT
MOTHER-DAUGHTER
RELATIONSHIP
JOURNAL

THE
DIFFICULT
MOTHER-DAUGHTER
RELATIONSHIP
JOURNAL

A Guide For Revealing & Healing
Toxic Generational Patterns

KAREN C.L. ANDERSON

mango
CORAL GABLES

Cover Design: Elina Diaz
Layout & Design: Elina Diaz

Mango is an active supporter of authors' rights to free speech and artistic expression in their books. The purpose of copyright is to encourage authors to produce exceptional works that enrich our culture and our open society.

Disclaimer: The author is not a licensed professional. This book details the author's personal experience and opinions. Among other things, it includes the author's reactions and memories. The author acknowledges others may remember or have experienced certain situations she recounts in this book differently than she does.

For permission requests, please contact the publisher at:
Mango Publishing Group
2850 S Douglas Road, 2nd Floor
Coral Gables, FL 33134 USA
info@mango.bz

For special orders, quantity sales, course adoptions and corporate sales, please email the publisher at sales@mango.bz. For trade and wholesale sales, please contact Ingram Publisher Services at customer.service@ingramcontent.com or +1.800.509.4887.

The Difficult Mother-Daughter Relationship Journal: A Guide For Revealing & Healing Toxic Generational Patterns

Library of Congress Cataloging-in-Publication number: 2019948632
ISBN: (print) 9781642501308, (ebook) 978-1-64250-131-5
BISAC category code: FAM033000—FAMILY & RELATIONSHIPS / Parenting / Parent & Adult Child

Printed in the United States of America

This book is dedicated to women in all their glorious forms and to painful generational patterns that want to be healed.

It is dedicated to all the women who have come before us, who sacrificed their spirits and their dreams because the world didn't value them as they were and as they wished to be.

It is dedicated to the fierce, wild, liberated women who will come after us.

"All the eggs a woman will ever carry form in her ovaries while she is a four-month-old fetus in the womb of her mother. This means our cellular life as an egg begins in the womb of our grandmother. Each of us spent five months in our grandmother's womb, and she in turn formed in the womb of her grandmother. We vibrate to the rhythm of our mother's blood before she herself is born, and this pulse is the thread of blood that runs all the way back through the grandmothers to the first mother."

—Layne Redmond, *When the Drummers Were Women*

Table of Contents

Preface

On a day that would normally be filled with busyness and family, my husband was in bed with what we thought was the flu (it wasn't…and he's fine) and I was zoning out on Facebook.

A message request came through from a woman who wrote, "Have you ever thought of writing a book called *Great Mothers, Difficult Adult Daughters*? I feel there is just far too much mother blaming and mother shaming in this world today."

(She was reacting to the title of my previous book, *Difficult Mothers, Adult Daughters: A Guide For Separation, Liberation & Inspiration*.)

She had a few other choice words and an accusation: "You are preying on vulnerable adult daughters who aren't taking responsibility for their appalling behavior to their mothers who love them unconditionally, who gave their all for their beloved daughters."

I noticed feelings arise in me. Defensiveness, anger…fear, even. A weight on my solar plexus. I also rolled my eyes.

I took a deep breath and responded. Kindly but honestly. I expressed that my work isn't about blame or fault for mothers *or* daughters. It's about taking responsibility for oneself.

She had more accusations.

I responded with a recommendation: Dr. Joshua Coleman is an expert on family estrangement and is the author of *When Parents Hurt*.

"He's okay. Not that good," she replied.

(Which I suspect is because, like me, he asks his readers to consider looking inward and to take responsibility for themselves, and many mothers and daughters are not ready to hear or do that…I know because I used to be that daughter.)

She continued, "You have to realize that I am both a mother and a daughter."

"Yes, I do realize that."

She went on to say that going no-contact (estrangement) is always wrong. I disagreed.

She told me that her father had been a "complete nightmare" yet she "stuck with him."

I shared that it was only when I took time and space away from my mother in order to better know and understand myself, that I was able to reinitiate contact from a healthier place.

She told me it was wrong of me. No matter what. I disagreed.

I asked her to tell me about her family. She asked me about mine.

She told me about her daughter who is choosing not to be in contact with her family. I told her a little bit about my relationship with my mother and the strained relationship she had with her mother.

And just like that, we became two women on two different continents sharing Christmas Day in an unlikely way.

Which isn't to say we ended our correspondence on a happy note. She was scared, hurt, and angry. Her fear, hurt, and anger weren't mine to address.

But I could hold space for possibility.

It was then that I knew I wanted to create guided journal for both mothers and adult daughters…for all women and anyone who identifies as a woman.

How many times have you said a version of one of the following phrases to yourself? "It stops with me! I won't treat my daughter the way my mother treated me," "My mother died, but she's still controlling me from the grave," "My daughter has changed. I no longer know who she is," "I am so tired of living in reaction to my mother," "She doesn't respect me or my boundaries!"

You're not alone. Studies suggest that nearly 30 percent of women have been estranged from their mothers at some point, which suggests that the number of women who struggle in their relationship with their mother or daughter (but aren't estranged) is even higher.

It has been considered shameful and taboo to discuss the pain of dysfunctional mother-daughter issues outside of lofty clinical pathologies and personality disorders, unless it's in a private support group where, often, the "support" keeps women stuck in painful stories, reactions, and patterns of behavior. In that paradigm, affected women are stuck conveying "lesser versions" of themselves, which, ironically, is often what happens between mothers and daughters who have a failing or dysfunctional relationship.

What was considered normal and okay in past generations (using fear, shame, authoritarianism, punishment, "should-ing," control, binary ways of thinking, and physical violence as parenting tools, not to mention the disallowance of being able to feel and express emotion) is now known to be abusive and traumatic.

The toxic generational patterns I mention in the title of this book? Their roots run in patriarchy, misogyny, and white supremacy. This is the trauma that runs deep in our DNA. It is what was unconsciously passed down through our maternal lineages, and we now hold it in our bodies.

This is what's at the heart of most mother-daughter conflict.

How we choose to heal individually is how we will heal collectively.

MUCH, MUCH LOVE,
KAREN

Introduction

Who is this guided journal for?

It's for you if…

- You struggle in your relationship with your mother and want it to be better.

- You struggle in your relationship with your daughter…she's changed, and you don't understand her anymore.

- You wish to no longer be in contact with your mother, without guilt.

- You are estranged from your daughter, not by your choice.

- You are estranged from your mother and you either no longer want to feel badly about it or want to reestablish contact but don't know how.

- You are the mother of a daughter and want to "break the cycle."

- She has died, and you have unresolved pain in regards to your relationship with her.

Note: If you are actively processing trauma, some of the prompts and practices in this journal may be triggering. Please seek out therapy if this applies to you. The "Resources" section on page 149 includes the websites of organizations where you can find therapists and other practitioners who specialize in such modalities as EMDR (Eye Movement Desensitization and Reprocessing therapy), somatic experiencing, Internal Family Systems, and others.

This guided journal includes insights, prompts, and practices that will help you…

- Access your own wisdom.

- Better see and understand the painful patterns that have come to you and through you via your maternal lineage.

- Heal those patterns so they no longer create suffering.

- Have a relationship built on healthy interdependence rather than dysfunctional codependence (assuming she is capable, which she very well may not be and that is not your fault or your responsibility).

- Set and maintain healthy boundaries.

- Accept what is, as is, even if she isn't ready for what you want.

As you work your way through this guided journal, let yourself know what you know, want what you want, and not want what you don't want.

Don't underestimate the simplicity of the prompts and practices. Each one builds on the previous one and represents your on-going evolution, guiding you to more of what you want in your life and relationships, not just with her, but with yourself and in the greater world.

Writing is powerful, and it's good for you. It helps you acknowledge, cope with, and resolve that which you struggle with. It's both the medicine and the sugar.

Writing clarifies, reduces stress, helps you solve problems from an intuitive, creative place, and helps you integrate what you're learning. It's one thing to consume information—it's another to act on it.

It takes courage to do this work. Intense emotions may come up as you make your way through the journal. You might find yourself feeling everything from guilt to anger to grief, but I hope you will also experience joy, laughter, and relief.

Note: If doing any of these practices is uncomfortable or distressful in any way, stop. Also, know what I share in this book can be an effective companion to therapy, but it is not a replacement for it. If you are in therapy, you may want to share these practices with your therapist.

Answers

Should I do this with her?

No. You can, of course, but I suggest you do the work on your own, at least at first.

Does she have to be alive?

No. This isn't so much about the two of you as it is about you making some choices about how you want to show up in the world. This is about your future, and not just in relation to her (whether she's alive or not). If she is no longer here, shift the tense of the questions to suit the situation.

I don't want to have to talk to/see/interact with her. Are you going to suggest that I should?

Absolutely not. For some women, choosing to not have her in their lives is the very best choice. You can, however, make these kinds of choices from a loving, proactive, powerful place, not from a reactive, defensive place, *for your own sake*. There is an option to reinitiate contact if that is what makes sense for you, and this guided journal will help you decide and take the appropriate action.

She is/was abusive and violent. Am I supposed to forgive and forget?

No. This work isn't about putting up with or approving of any type of abuse, whether it happened long ago or is happening now. It's about learning how to tell the story about what happened in such a way that it no longer hurts or minimizes you, but rather empowers and liberates you. It's about learning how to establish healthy limits and boundaries (up to and including no longer seeing or speaking to her).

Forgiveness is a concept that is misunderstood and too often applied in situations where one or both parties aren't ready. Don't force or shame yourself into forgiving. Work toward developing your own standards of what is okay or not okay, based on your values (there are plenty of prompts in the journal that will help you do just that).

The only forgiveness I recommend is self-forgiveness.

She is/has [insert addiction, mental illness, or personality disorder]. This won't work because of that. She doesn't or seemingly can't respect my boundaries.

It may not work for *her*. She doesn't have to do it, and she doesn't have to know that you are doing it. Her disrespect doesn't mean that boundaries don't work…or that you'll be a failure at setting them. It simply means you are being invited to respect yourself.

How is this guided journal different than *Difficult Mothers, Adult Daughters: A Guide for Separation, Liberation & Inspiration*?

This journal is designed to help you create a reference for yourself, based on your needs, values, wants, and preferences, not hers. And while this book includes some of the same prompts and practices, it expands on them and includes many more. It also opens the door to mothers who wish to take a deep look inside. I wanted it to be more inclusive, to bridge greater understanding, and to create healing on both micro and macro levels.

If you are interested in my guidance as you work through this journal, please send me an email: karen@kclanderson.com. I offer one-on-one coaching to mothers and daughters (separately or together).

Guidelines

1. Give yourself as much time as you need/want. There's no rush.

2. Engage with compassionate objectivity, and examine yourself and your relationship with fascination and curiosity, rather than harsh judgment, shame, and guilt.

3. Don't judge what comes through. Don't censor or analyze your words or yourself as you write.

4. When a prompt asks you to consider your thoughts, keep this in mind:

Thoughts are simply the 50,000 to 70,000 interpretations, sentences, judgments, and opinions that run through your brain every day, all day. They are merely sounds, words, stories, and bits of language.

5. When a prompt asks you to consider your emotions, how you feel or felt, keep this in mind:

Emotions are energy in motion—vibrations in your body that you can feel physically—that are usually described in one word. Happy. Sad. Angry. Scared. Happiness has a vibration. Anger has a vibration. Sadness has a vibration. Fear has a vibration.

So when asked how you feel or felt, take a moment to quiet your mind, tap into the sensations in your body, and use one or two simple feeling words.

For example:

> *I felt grief.*
>
> *I felt delight.*
>
> *I felt enraged.*

Note: *I felt like she should have known better.* Or: *I felt that she was disrespectful.* These are thoughts.

6. If she is no longer here—that is, if she has died—change the question and or tense of the question to reflect that.

7. For simplicity's sake, from here on out, rather than overusing the words "mother" and "daughter" I will mostly use the words "her" and "she," which you can apply to your particular situation.

Intend

Intend (verb): to direct the mind on

No matter where you are in your relationship with her, whether she is alive or not, whether you speak to her or not, your intention is important because it will serve as a touchstone throughout this guided journal.

Try not to think of your intention as a goal. Your intention is more about who you want to be in the relationship and in the world versus what you want do or a specific outcome that involves her.

There's an old saying: be careful what you wish for. I'd like to state it this way: be clear and honest about what you want.

Don't intend something because you think it's what you should want.

Want what you want.

Don't want what you don't want.

Most of all, remember that your intention is for you, not her. She has her own intentions.

Why did you buy this book?

_____

_____

_____

_____

_____

_____

_____

_____

_____

_____

What are you hoping to accomplish?

_____

_____

_____

_____

_____

_____

_____

_____

Do you think you will be successful? Why or why not?

_____

_____

_____

_____

_____

_____

_____

_____

_____

_____

What do you think needs to happen in order for you to succeed?

_____

_____

_____

_____

_____

What are your hopes?

_____

_____

_____

_____

What are your fears?

_____

_____

_____

_____

_____

Imagine yourself standing in front of her (whether she's alive or not). How do you feel? How do you *want* to feel?

_____

_____

_____

_____

_____

_____

_____

_____

_____

What do you think needs to happen in order for it to be this way?

_____

_____

_____

_____

What don't you want?

_____

_____

_____

_____

_____

If you could wave a magic wand and change three things about your relationship with her, what would they be?

_____

_____

_____

_____

On a regular basis, how would you like to feel (pick three emotions)?

_____

_____

_____

_____

What do you want to bring with you into the future?

_____

_____

_____

_____

What do you want to leave behind?

_____

_____

_____

_____

_____

Who do you want to be in this relationship?

_____

_____

_____

_____

_____

How do you want to show up?

_____

_____

_____

_____

_____

If your intention could talk to you, what would it say?

_____

_____

_____

_____

_____

Based on everything you've written down so far, what is your intention?

_____

_____

_____

_____

_____

Simply notice what came up as a result of answering these questions. Jot down some notes if you want to.

Now? Detach yourself from a specific result or outcome, and let your journaling do the work. What does this look like in practical terms? You have created a written intention. It is being held for you. Trust in that, and turn the page.

Reveal

Reveal (verb): make (previously unknown information) known

> "If you look deeply into the palm of your hand, you will see your parents and all generations of your ancestors. All of them are alive in this moment. Each is present in your body. You are the continuation of each of these people."
>
> —Thich Nhat Hanh

Your direct maternal lineage is the line that follows your mother's maternal ancestry. This line consists entirely of women. And those women had all kinds of experiences. There is most likely unconscious fear and collective trauma in your maternal lineage. There are patterns and wounds that have been passed down to you.

Here are some common ways these patterns and wounds can show up:

- You compare and despair.

- You feel stuck, overwhelmed, and like an under-achiever.

- Or you are over-achieving, but without any joy or fulfillment, just going through the motions in an effort to prove your worth.

- Shame, blame, guilt, and desperation.

- Fear of failure.

- Fear of success (believe it or not): believing that if you succeed you won't be loved, someone will disapprove, or that you're somehow "showing off."

- Putting up with bad behavior in others.

- Constantly seeking approval, validation, and permission from outside yourself (and especially from her).

- People-pleasing and being afraid to say "no."

- Taking on other people's problems and thinking it's on you to fix them.

- Self-sabotage (especially when you get close to achieving something).

- Binge eating, binge drinking, binge shopping, binge anything.

- Feeling chronically frustrated, angry, and maybe even enraged.

- Trying to control the uncontrollable.

- Chronic worry and anxiety.

- Chronic overwhelm, confusion, and hopelessness.

- Believing it is selfish or narcissistic to put yourself first, or even to love, accept, or care for yourself.

- Believing it is your responsibility to take care of others, emotionally speaking.

- Thinking that your desires and preferences don't matter.

- Not having a clear sense of who you are and what you want.

- And if you *do* know what you want, feeling incapable of doing or having it.

- Having weak or non-existent boundaries.

- Being afraid to speak your truth and take up space.

What do you know about the women who came before you?

_____

_____

_____

_____

_____

_____

What did your mother tell you about her childhood?

_____

_____

_____

_____

_____

What did she tell you about her life when she was a young woman?

_____

_____

_____

_____

_____

_____

What do you know about her relationship with her mother?

_____

_____

_____

_____

_____

_____

What do you know about her dreams and disappointments?

_____

_____

_____

_____

_____

_____

Or maybe she didn't tell you, and that in and of itself tells you something?

_____

_____

_____

_____

_____

_____

What did others tell you about her?

_____

_____

_____

_____

_____

_____

Did you see any of the patterns and wounds listed on the previous page in her life?

_____

_____

_____

_____

_____

_____

How did those patterns and wounds show up?

_____

_____

_____

_____

_____

_____

What else stands out when you think about her life?

_____

_____

_____

_____

_____

_____

Jot down anything that comes to mind.

_____

_____

_____

_____

_____

_____

_____

_____

_____

_____

Write a mini-autobiography. Anything that comes to mind is worth putting on the page. Don't censor yourself. Let your pen (or keyboard) take your mind where it wants to go. Include any or all of the following:

What's your story?

Who are your parents?

When and where were you born?

What were you told about that time?

What's your earliest memory?

Do you know the first word you ever said?

Do you have siblings?

What stands out about your childhood?

Where did you go to school?

Who were your friends?

Did you like school?

What was your favorite subject?

What were your hopes and dreams?

Who did you date?

Did you go to college?

What kinds of jobs have you had?

What do you enjoy doing for fun?

Are you married?

Divorced?

Do you have children?

What are your greatest disappointments?

Triumphs?

Fears?

Struggles?

Most profound moments?

What else?

Going back to that list of patterns and wounds, which ones do you struggle with? Are they the same ones your mother struggled with?

_____

_____

_____

_____

_____

_____

_____

_____

_____

_____

_____

_____

Reveal

Reveal

_____

_____

_____

_____

_____

_____

Now tell the story of your relationship with her. It doesn't have to be linear. Write down as many details as you can. Again, don't censor yourself.

If you're a mother, you can start with your desire to have a child, at conception, or when she was born. Whatever feels right.

If you're a daughter, you can start with your earliest memories of your mother.

Write about the hard things. The fights, the disappointments, the hurt. Write down what she did or didn't do; what she should have done; what she shouldn't have done; how your life would have been different if it had or hadn't happened.

Write it all down. Get the whole thing out of your head.

_____

_____

_____

_____

_____

_____

_____

_____

_____

_____

_____

_____

Thinking back on what you wrote so far...

What made you laugh?

_____

_____

_____

_____

_____

What made you cry?

_____

_____

_____

_____

_____

What made you angry?

_____

_____

_____

_____

_____

_____

What surprised you?

_____

_____

_____

_____

_____

What patterns did you notice?

_____

_____

_____

_____

_____

_____

Awareness

Awareness (noun): knowledge or perception of a situation, fact, or emotion. Consciousness, recognition, understanding.

Awareness is where healing starts.

The more aware you are, the more access you have to the wisdom within you. Intentionally cultivate awareness.

Consider that your mind/consciousness isn't simply your thoughts or what your brain does, but rather your entire nervous system, which includes your brain and your second brain (your gut), which are connected via the vagus nerve. I share this not as a biology lesson, but rather to illustrate that the whole of you is an interconnected system.

Your thoughts and feelings work in concert and are equally valuable and wise, despite what our culture teaches us: that thoughts, intellect (and action) are valued over feelings and emotions, which we've been taught to ignore. In the brain, there is no distinction between thoughts and feelings. They are the input for your brain and nervous system, interpretations for everything that happens in your environment.

For the purposes of this journal, however, it's helpful to make a distinction between thoughts, beliefs, emotions, and identity.

Thoughts are the tens of thousands of opinions and judgments that constantly run through your brain. They are words. Sometimes you are aware of them, sometimes you are not. Over the course of your life, your conscious and unconscious thoughts create and inform your beliefs and identity.

Beliefs and Identity are the state of mind in which you think something to be true based on who you believe yourself to be, with or without there any real proof. You are sometimes unconscious of your beliefs. While your thoughts help you form your beliefs and identity, your beliefs and identity continue to inform how and what you think, how you interpret your experiences, and how you feel about them. They are the lens through which you view the world. It sometimes seems like identities are set in stone and unchangeable.

Emotions are energy in motion—literal vibrations that you experience in your body (not your brain)—and they are often related to the thoughts you're thinking, what you believe about yourself and others, and the identity you have carved out for yourself. Your emotions often inform how you react, respond, and behave, and your behavior is often driven by your feelings.

Notice

Notice (verb): the act of paying attention

"This is the first, the wildest and the wisest thing I know: that the soul exists and is built entirely out of attentiveness."

—Mary Oliver

Instead of engaging with the things she does and says (or did and said), just look. Use awareness to simply observe. Pretend you are a scientist and your job is to see what's happening without having an opinion about it and without labeling it.

Pick a memory of her (or an interaction with her) that holds a charge for you.

_____

_____

_____

_____

_____

What did you observe back then?

_____

_____

_____

_____

_____

What are you observing now?

_____

_____

_____

_____

_____

What was your opinion about what you observed back then? What meaning did you give it?

_____

_____

_____

_____

_____

What's your opinion now? Has the meaning changed?

_____

_____

_____

_____

_____

What's the difference between simply observing, and observing and having opinions about what you see?

_____

_____

_____

_____

_____

Is there a difference between what she did or said, and how you labeled her behavior?

_____

_____

_____

_____

What's the effect on you, personally?

_____

_____

_____

_____

What urges did you have in regards to what you observed and noticed?

_____

_____

_____

_____

_____

How did you respond or react to those urges?

_____

_____

_____

_____

_____

How did it feel to notice and observe without engaging or having an opinion?

_____

_____

_____

_____

_____

What are the opinions, thoughts, and judgments that ran through your head in regards to what you observed and noticed?

_____

_____

_____

_____

In the moment you were reacting to what she was doing or saying, what was happening in your brain?

_____

_____

_____

_____

_____

You are fascinating and you deserve your own compassionate curiosity. Instead of judging yourself for having opinions, thoughts, judgments, and reactions, simply take a deep breath and repeat after me: "I am a fascinating human being. My brain is so interesting to me."

Feel

Feel (verb): to perceive by a physical vibration or sensation

> "When you learn to feel your feelings you are showing your brain and body that you are safe, that there is no threat to your survival, and that you can handle any situation."
>
> —Christie Inge

One unhelpful pattern that often gets passed down via our maternal lineage is the disallowance of being able to feel and express emotion. This is the essence of trauma: the disconnection of our bodies from our emotions.

This is why emotions are one of the most misunderstood of all human experiences.

What else defines emotions?

Emotions are vibrations in your body that you can feel physically—that are usually described in one word. Happy. Sad. Angry. Scared. Happiness has a vibration. Anger has a vibration. Sadness has a vibration. Fear has a vibration.

Emotions are not thoughts or ideas. They are not concepts with long, vague descriptions. They are not opinions or judgments.

Sometimes, emotional vibrations are uncomfortable. Allowing yourself to feel an uncomfortable emotion won't hurt you or anyone else. The earth won't open up and swallow you whole, nor will you explode into a million pieces.

Acting on emotions without consideration is a different story.

While emotions themselves are not thoughts or ideas, they are often informed by your identity, beliefs, and thoughts. Something happens and your mind (made up of both your brain and your nervous system) assesses what happened and assigns meaning to it. That meaning then informs how you feel. All of this happens in an instant, usually without your awareness.

This is what it means to be human. To be alive.

You can reconnect with your emotions in a healthy way. Here's my process:

1. Notice. You notice the pit in your stomach, the prickle of heat on your face, your breathing becomes shallow, you feel expansiveness in your chest, your throat gets tight, your knees turn to jelly. And so on.

2. Don't judge or assign meaning to these sensations (especially if they're uncomfortable). If you judge yourself or your emotions, you won't be as willing to feel them. You will distract, deny, pretend, stuff, resist, or otherwise react. When you allow emotion to be present without judgment, you will be able to feel and experience it.

3. Allow the emotion to just be there. Stay present with it. Notice the urge to distract or resist. Bring yourself back. Release the resistance and allow the feeling to be there.

4. Describe it in detail (more on this on the following page). Where is it in your body? What color is it? Does it have a texture? A temperature? Some other quality? Does it change the more you focus on it and describe it? How? Experience the emotion while at the same time describing yourself experiencing the emotion. (Note: you are not describing what you're thinking or why you're feeling what you're feeling—you are simply describing what's going on in your body.)

5. Name it. The more specific you can get, the better. Angry. Gleeful. Frustrated. Ashamed. Annoyed. Rage. Ambivalent. Ecstatic. Jealous. Anguished. Naming it allows your mind to make sense of what your body is experiencing. For help with this, visit the Atlas of Emotions website (http://atlasofemotions.org/).

6. Be willing to feel it. For two minutes. That's it.

7. Be curious and fascinated about what you just experienced. Ask yourself what message your emotion had for you. As with most intense emotion, the message is usually from the past: the feeling isn't new, it's an old emotion that you've stuffed, and something triggered it.

8. Take responsibility for your emotions. Your emotions are yours, not hers. You're the one feeling it, and you are the one responsible for it.

Here are examples of *not* taking responsibility for emotions.

- She makes me so angry!

- When you're good, you make me happy.

- She should know better than to push my buttons.

- I need you to be happy so I can be happy.

- It's their fault I'm angry.

9. Choose a safe way to express the emotion either alone or with someone who won't interrupt the process or keep you mired in the emotion. If your body feels like moving, let it move. Let it lead you. Notice if you want to stomp your feet because you're honoring your body's guidance on how to move the energy or if you're doing it because you're trying to avoid the emotion.

Move through all the steps of feeling without interruption. Humans are adept at interrupting themselves in the middle of the process. We don't like struggling—and others don't like watching us struggle—with intense emotion, so we/they try and talk us out of it, or somehow save us from it, because they're trying to make themselves feel better. And we do the same to/for them.

And when we do, we also diminish resilience, miss the wisdom, and delay emotional maturity.

When you allow yourself to move through all the steps without judgment, you not only feel better but are able to mobilize and show yourself how resilient you actually are. You can melt down as you accept emotions, and this causes you to thrive.

Avoiding, ignoring, resisting, interrupting, intercepting, stuffing, distracting, distrusting, and intellectualizing emotions will make them unconscious and chronic. This is how you hurt yourself (and sometimes others) with your emotions. Complaining, wallowing, and stewing, are really just another way of resisting emotion. It's more profound to acknowledge and feel an emotion, rather than saying, "I'm past that."

To paraphrase Brené Brown: Instead of acting out your hurt, feel your hurt. Instead of inflicting pain on others, acknowledge your own pain. Instead of living disappointed, risk feeling disappointed.

What emotion are you experiencing right now?

_____

_____

_____

_____

How do you know?

_____

_____

_____

_____

Where is the emotion located in your body?

_____

_____

_____

_____

What color is it?

_____

_____

_____

_____

_____

Is it hard or soft?

_____

_____

_____

_____

_____

Is it fast or slow?

_____

_____

_____

_____

What other qualities does it have?

_____

_____

_____

_____

_____

What else can you say about how it feels?

_____

_____

_____

_____

_____

How does this emotion make you want to react? What does it make you want to do?

_____

_____

_____

_____

_____

What judgments do you have about this emotion?

_____

_____

_____

_____

_____

What do you make this emotion mean about you?

_____

_____

_____

_____

_____

Why are you experiencing this emotion right now?

_____

_____

_____

_____

What is the thought or belief that goes with this emotion?

_____

_____

_____

_____

Think about a time when you believed she caused you to experience a negative emotion, and write down what she did or said.

_____

_____

_____

_____

_____

What was the emotion you felt?

_____

_____

_____

_____

_____

What is the thought you are thinking that is causing this emotion?

_____

_____

_____

_____

_____

What would it be like to take responsibility for this emotion?

_____

_____

_____

_____

_____

What is the benefit of taking responsibility for it?

_____

_____

_____

_____

_____

Make a list of emotions you associate with her and your relationship with her. For each one, actually take the time to summon the vibration in your body and then describe it. Play with it, and notice how you can increase it and decrease it at will.

_____

_____

_____

_____

_____

What's the worst emotion you can imagine having to feel in regards to your relationship with her?

_____

_____

_____

_____

_____

What would it feel like in your body? Get specific with it. Where in your body would it be? Describe it. What would it feel like, literally?

_____

_____

_____

_____

_____

Why would you not want to experience this feeling? Why would you try to avoid or resist it?

_____

_____

_____

_____

_____

If you were willing to feel this emotion without resistance, what would be different?

_____

_____

_____

_____

_____

How might you show up in your relationship with her?

_____

_____

_____

_____

_____

Tend

Tend (verb): to care for or look after; give one's attention to

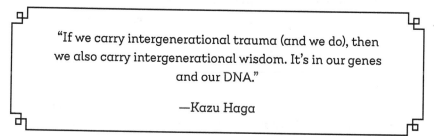

"If we carry intergenerational trauma (and we do), then we also carry intergenerational wisdom. It's in our genes and our DNA."

—Kazu Haga

It's time to get into your body. To reconnect with yourself. To tend to yourself.

There are many ways to do this, some of which you may already be doing and which may already serve you:

- Yoga

- Breathwork

- Singing

- Chanting

- Playing wind instruments

- Guided meditation

- Somatic work

- Emotional Freedom Techniques (a.k.a. "tapping")

Here are four simple exercises I practice myself that come from the field of Somatic Experiencing ®. I am not a licensed or certified SE™ professional, and the practices I share here can be found in various places on the Internet. Please also check the resources section of this book for more information.

Note: If doing any of these practices is uncomfortable or distressful in any way, stop. Also, know what I share in this book can be an effective companion to therapy, but it is not a replacement for it. If you are in therapy, you may want to share these practices with your therapist.

1. Affirm yourself and your presence. "I am here-. My name is
_____. It is [date, time], and I am here [location]."

Notice how it feels in your body to do this. Try it standing up and see how it changes. Notice what your body wants to do as you affirm yourself and your presence.

2. Orient yourself. This can be done when you're calm, and it can be done when you're stressed or in stressful situations or environments.

Sit as comfortably as you can, and let your attention wander around your space. Notice what attracts your attention and draws your interest. Pick three things and say, out loud or inside your head, each thing as your eyes focus on it.

For example, as I write this, I am sitting in my home office. I sat back and let my eyes wander. I noticed and said to myself, "There's the Scorpio print that was made for me in Italy. And the photo of my husband that I love so much. And the blanket, which is about to fall off the chair."

Then, move your attention inward and notice what attracts your attention there. Notice sensations: urges to move, tightness, softness, pressure, etc. Name them and see how they evolve.

"My shoulders are scrunched up, I am breathing shallowly, and I can feel a tenseness in my lower back."

Don't judge your observations. Simply make a mental note of them. In this way, you will establish yourself in the here and now.

3. Hold yourself. This is a way to define your literal boundaries, and it has a calming effect on the nervous system.

Stand comfortably, and place your hands on either side of your head. You can apply a bit of pressure, or not. Imagine that you are molding a container for your thoughts. Feel the sensations on both your head and your hands.

Now move one hand to your forehead and the other to the back of your skull. Continue to notice the sensations and boundaries your hands are creating.

Move the hand on the back of your head to your heart, and keep the other hand on your forehead. What changes? Are there sensations between your two hands?

Now move the hand that was on your forehead to your belly and keep the other hand on your heart. Continue to feel and notice the sensations.

And finally, move one hand to your solar plexus and one to the base of your head, where you head and neck meet.

4. Express yourself. This combines a breathing exercise and a chant, much like the "Om" in yoga. The vibrations created when you sound or chant a deep "voo" (on the exhale) "tone" the vagus nerve. The longest nerve in your body, the vagus nerve has two main functions: it monitors all the major organs in your body and communicates with the brain stem, and it regulates social engagement, digestion, alertness/consciousness, and emotions.

To practice, inhale through your nose and as you exhale, make the "voo" sound (imagine a foghorn) in as low a tone as you can, making the effort to feel the vibrations in your lower abdomen.

After each round, close your eyes and sit calmly, noticing what you feel in your body.

These simple practices can expand the capacity of your nervous system and cue your body to know that it is safe. Why is this important in difficult mother-daughter relationships? There's likely trauma in your maternal lineage that gets in the way of having a healthier relationship.

Retell

Retell (verb): tell (a story) again or differently in order to heal

> "Owning our stories and loving ourselves through that
> process is the bravest thing we will ever do."
>
> —Brené Brown

In the "Reveal" section of this journal, you told your story. I define "story" as all the things you tell yourself (over and over again), about yourself, in regards to all the things that have happened in your life. This is partly how you created your identity.

When you are standing on your story, you share it in a powerful way. Powerful stories don't resist, deny, or hide a painful past. They simply reflect how you've grown and healed.

Because it's the truth.

You can acknowledge that you suffered without blaming yourself or her.

You can choose now to be responsible for your healing.

I will share one of my transformed stories: My parents were divorced when I was two. My unconscious beliefs about myself in regards to their divorce caused me much suffering well into adulthood.

My painful story was there must have been something deeply wrong with me that caused their divorce. I don't blame myself for this belief, because it's what children do. They make everything that is happening outside themselves mean something about them. But until fairly recently, no one was teaching us (on purpose) how to do this in a healthy way.

By choosing to delve deeply into the circumstances of my parents' lives, I have a much different understanding. Now my story is their marriage may have been ill-fated from the get-go, but they needed to get together long enough to bring me into the world. I am here now, and that's all that matters.

This doesn't mean I never, ever feel sadness or grief in regards to my past, but rather that I no longer make their divorce mean that something is wrong with me.

> "All sorrows can be born if you can put them into a story or tell a story about them."
>
> —Karen Blixen

Pick a painful memory in your relationship with her.

Using what you learned in the Awareness section (page 43), answer the following prompts:

What happened? Write down all the details.

_____

_____

_____

_____

_____

What were your thoughts about what happened then? What are they now?

_____

_____

_____

_____

_____

What are your beliefs about yourself that inform your thoughts?

_____

_____

_____

_____

_____

What did you tell yourself *about* yourself in response to what happened?

_____

_____

_____

_____

When you think about that, how do you feel?

_____

_____

_____

_____

Now write about how you behave when you feel that way. In other words, how do you show up in the world when you feel that way?

_____

_____

_____

_____

_____

Reminder: the purpose of this exercise is simply to reveal your whole self to yourself, not to punish yourself.

Use these prompts as a jumping-off point to explore other memories that stand out to you.

Powerful pattern-interrupting questions:

Who am I when I interact with her?

_____

_____

_____

_____

_____

Who do I want to be when I interact with her?

_____

_____

_____

_____

_____

What am I making it mean that she _____?

Why am I choosing to think that?

How do I want to feel now?

How do I want to feel about my past?

_____

_____

Is this thought helpful?

_____

_____

_____

_____

Is this the lens I want to be using to look at this situation?

_____

_____

_____

_____

What are my emotions showing me?

_____

_____

_____

_____

Am I acting from the belief that I am safe or that I am in danger?

_____

_____

_____

_____

_____

What happens when I respond this way instead of that way?

_____

_____

_____

_____

What do I believe about pain and discomfort?

_____

_____

_____

_____

What do I want to believe about it?

_____

_____

_____

_____

_____

What's the difference between pain and suffering?

_____

_____

_____

_____

_____

Who would I be without my "suffering" story?

_____

_____

_____

_____

_____

What else is true?

_____

_____

_____

_____

_____

If she's no longer here, answer the questions based on your experiences with her when she was alive.

Rather than resisting, trying to change, judging, or pushing away the thoughts that don't feel good, just notice them. Watch when those unwelcome thoughts show up, rather than beating yourself up for having them.

When you see a connection, it's tempting to want to change your thoughts (ex., recite "positive affirmations") so you can feel better. But "changing your thoughts" reactively is another form of resistance, judgment, and avoidance because underneath those negative thoughts are other thoughts like, "I shouldn't think that," or, "It's so deeply entrenched," or, "UGH I hate that I have these negative thoughts."

Being aware simply shows you the impact your thinking has on you.

It is possible to change thoughts and beliefs and to let go of identities that no longer serve you, and the first step is awareness. It then becomes a practice. Rather than trying to force it, be kind to yourself and let the process happen naturally and organically.

Forgive yourself for the things you told yourself about yourself that aren't really true about you. Imagine what it would feel like to stand on that story and tell it in a powerful and truthful way.

For the sake of this work, let's define forgiveness this way: Forgiveness is choosing to think differently in order to feel better. That's all. Nothing more, nothing less.

When you think about yourself now, in relation to her, what are the most common emotions you feel?

_____

_____

_____

_____

_____

How would you like to feel?

_____

_____

_____

_____

_____

Revisit your intention.

_____

_____

_____

_____

_____

Has it changed? It's okay if it has.

_____

_____

_____

_____

_____

Betray

Betray (verb): break or violate a presumptive contract, trust, or confidence that produces moral and psychological conflict within a relationship

> "...I want to know if you can disappoint another to be true to yourself. If you can bear the accusation of betrayal and not betray your own soul..."
>
> —Oriah Mountain Dreamer, poem "The Invitation"

Difficult mother-daughter relationships are based on unhealthy contracts: the unspoken and often unconscious "rules" and "shoulds." These contracts arise from the needs and expectations that mothers and daughters don't communicate but hold each other accountable for anyway. They are silent and often unconscious, which makes them hard to see and address.

Here are some examples:

I won't become too successful, because I am afraid she'll feel threatened.

I will always put her needs first.

Her needs are more important than mine.

She knows what's best for me.

I need her to tell me what to do.

I need her to reflect back to me that I am a good mother.

I need her approval so I know I am a good daughter.

She needs to be successful the way I define it, so I don't look bad.

I didn't raise her to be this way.

What agreements or contracts do you have with her that you didn't realize?

_____

_____

_____

_____

_____

What are the shoulds and shouldn'ts you have for her? Make a list.

_____

_____

_____

_____

_____

Why should or shouldn't she _____?

_____

_____

_____

_____

_____

If she behaved the way you wanted her to, how would that change the way you think about her? Feel about her? Get specific here. What thoughts would you have, and what emotions would you feel.

_____

_____

_____

_____

_____

Do you want her to behave this way even if she doesn't want to? Why or why not?

_____

_____

_____

_____

When she wants you to act a certain way so she can feel good, what is that like for you?

_____

_____

_____

_____

In what ways has she made you responsible for her feelings?

_____

_____

_____

_____

In what ways have you made her responsible for your feelings?

_____

_____

_____

_____

_____

Notice, in your day-to-day interactions, when you find yourself thinking about what she should and shouldn't do or say, not to mention when you "should" on yourself.

∼

Here is a list of things you might believe you owe her (or that she may think you owe her…or that you may think she owes you):

- Being a "positive" reflection of her (meaning, her definition of "positive")

- Secrecy

- Emotional care-taking

- Physical care-taking

- Tolerating "bad" behavior

- An explanation of why you choose to live your life differently than she does

- Your agreement with everything she believes

- Having the same values

- A lack of boundaries

- Success (meaning, her definition of "success")

- Failure ("don't outshine me")

- Hugs
- Kisses
- Phone calls
- Texts
- Visits
- Happiness
- Unhappiness ("misery loves company")
- Money
- Time

Consciously and cleanly choosing to *give* any of these things versus unconsciously giving or expecting them is the difference between interdependence and dysfunctional codependence.

～

What contracts and agreements do you want to have?

_____

_____

_____

_____

_____

What contracts and agreements do you want to betray or break in the name of creating a healthier relationship?

_____

_____

_____

"What if forgiveness is neutral? How might we learn to forgive ourselves for not measuring up to some artificial, inherited, or inauthentic ideal of how relationships/family should act?"

—Tami Dew Rich

In April 2015, Elizabeth Gilbert wrote a Facebook post about tribal shame and the work of Dr. Mario Martinez, who wrote a book called *The Mind-Body Code*. He studies the ways our thoughts and emotions affect our physical health, and he is particularly interested in the harmful ways shame affects the mind and body.

In her post, Gilbert outlined an exercise Dr. Martinez created to help people liberate themselves from fear and shame and it occurred to me you might find this exercise helpful.

Step 1: Sit quietly, and allow your mind and your breathing to settle. Acknowledge you need(ed) to abandon her in order to live your life the way you want. Acknowledge that she felt/will feel betrayed.

Step 2: Say, aloud: "_____, I am going to abandon you now. I am going to betray you now."

Liz says this is powerful because you are saying the opposite of what you have probably spent your life trying to prove: you haven't betrayed or abandoned your her. You may have even made yourself sick trying to prove you are loyal, you have done nothing wrong, you haven't changed.

But it doesn't work, because she doesn't believe you. Because she knows (and you know, too) that when you chose a different way for yourself, you betrayed and abandoned her. You changed because you needed to. You left her behind because that was the only way to become the person you were meant to be.

And? It's ALL good. Why? Because it doesn't mean you don't love her.

As Liz said, *"this exercise has nothing to do with love."* You can always love her. This exercise is about breaking the spell of shame, and the only way to do that is to take ownership of your life and to admit to the consequences of leaving her values behind.

Step 3: Become her (in your mind). Say to yourself (in her voice) these words: *"I completely understand. I forgive you. All I want is for you to be happy."*

It's important you hold both sides of this imagined conversation.

Step 4: Rebuild what Dr. Martinez calls your own "field of honor."

Shaming works because it attacks your sense of honor. "Every tribe is governed by its own code of honor, and once you have broken that honor code, the tribe will accuse you (overtly or subtly) of having no honor at all. This accusation is what makes you sick. This is what makes you suffer," Liz Gilbert writes.

So you must rebuild your own field of honor in order to make yourself healthy again.

You do this by making a list of all the times you have been honorable, starting as young as you can remember. What was the first honorable act of your life? Go from there and write down all the ways in which you have been honorable.

Step 5: Feel righteous anger (and note here that I am not suggesting that you act on it…just *feel* it).

You will know you are standing in your field of honor when your first reaction to attempts to shaming you are righteous anger. You will know you are on the road to emotional health and recovery when she tries to shame you, and rather than absorb that shame, you instead react with righteous anger.

Dr. Martinez suggests there is a role in your life for healthy anger, for appropriate anger, for righteous anger. Righteous anger is a fast, hot fire that burns up the poison of shaming and protects your field of honor. This is the anger that rises up like a dragon and says, "Don't you DARE try to shame me!" This anger is correct, just, and fair. You are entitled to it. You must claim it.

You are a person of honor who does not deserve to be shamed. Righteous anger protects you from judging yourself when she tries to shame you so learn how to *feel* it when and if you experience shaming.

Repeat after me: "I do not deserve to be shamed!"

Practice as often as you need.

Delve

Delve (verb): to examine a subject in detail (and, interestingly, the noun "delve" means cave)

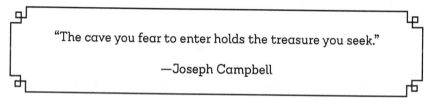

"The cave you fear to enter holds the treasure you seek."

—Joseph Campbell

The relationship you have with yourself—your whole self—will inform and impact the relationship you have with her. If you can't honor your whole self, it makes it harder to hold space for and accept her whole self (not that this is a requirement).

What does it mean to be "whole"? For me, it's when I choose to unflinchingly see and acknowledge the parts of myself that make my face prickle with hot shame, love myself through it, and ultimately reclaim and integrate those parts.

There's no more resistance to any part of myself. No more hiding. No more people-pleasing because if-they-really-knew-me-they-wouldn't-like-me.

"Good" is when I have a mask on and am denying, resisting, or hiding the parts of myself that I find disgusting or ugly.

Choosing to unflinchingly see and acknowledge the parts of yourself that make your face prickle with hot shame, and then choosing to love yourself through it? That's freedom right there.

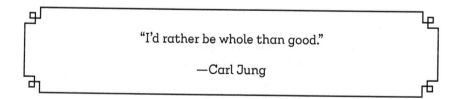

"I'd rather be whole than good."

—Carl Jung

Pick one thing she thinks about you and maybe even has said to you that you find offensive, and write it down.

Ask yourself why it's important to you that she not think or say this (you can go deeper and ask yourself why it's important that she approve of you in this specific situation).

Do you believe what she thinks or says about you is true? If yes, why?

Do you believe what she thinks or says about you is negative or bad? If yes, why?

What do you want to believe about yourself in regards to this thing she thinks or says?

How does it feel to believe that?

Reframe it. "She thinks or said [insert whatever she said here]. I don't agree with her, nor do I think that [insert whatever she said here] is a bad thing. What I want to believe is [insert what you believe here]."

Can you find evidence for what you want to believe? Write it down.

_____

_____

_____

_____

_____

(This exercise comes from Christie Inge's Shadow & Light course, with her permission, which you can find here: christieinge.com/sal-ecourse.)

Imagine you are in the passenger seat of a car driving down the highway. As you look out the window, you notice there are billboards with your picture on them and descriptions about who and what you are.

Make a list of all the things you'd be embarrassed or ashamed of, guilty about, or otherwise afraid to see said about you on those billboards:

Now you've met your shadow, write down one thing you want to do/create/be.

Then, considering all the things you wrote down in response to the billboard prompt, ask yourself how those things keep you from doing/creating/being the thing you really want to do/create/be.

What are the words we use to describe shame? Why do people (especially mothers and daughters) hate the idea of reading about themselves?

- Arrogant
- Self-Centered
- Selfish
- Stupid
- Greedy
- Hypocritical
- Ordinary
- Untalented
- A Fraud
- Dishonest
- Liar
- Spoiled
- Worthless
- Pathetic
- Disorganized
- Unprofessional
- Lazy
- Needy
- Desperate
- Controlling
- Etc.

What parts of yourself are you rejecting?

_____

_____

_____

_____

What part are you not looking at because you're afraid if you look, you'll have to change?

_____

_____

_____

_____

How do you come to accept these traits you fear she will see in you or call you?

_____

_____

_____

_____

Start by acknowledging the reason you fear this particular judgment.

Acknowledge all humans have the capacity for all human emotion and behavior.

Acknowledge you are human.

Acknowledge that, perhaps, you are that trait you fear she'll see, at least a little.

Find the good side of that trait.

Is there something that you can accept as part of who you are? Once you do, do you see how that frees you up to do what you do and not worry about that label? Find the judgment or shame word you fear, and find a way to fully, and actually, embrace it.

We all have times when we're brilliant and times when we aren't. This is why shadow work is so powerful: understanding and accepting the times you are [pick a word from your list here] as part of who you are is how you can, at other times, be the opposite.

~

Here's an example of some shadow work I did several years ago:

Selfish, controlling, hypocritical, lazy, spoiled, know-it-all, petty, small-minded, mean, pathetic, liar.

These were the words I didn't want to see on billboards with my name and picture.

I had a visceral reaction to these words and to the meanings I gave them. They stung and my face prickled with hot shame when I thought about what it would be like to be called those things.

I challenged myself to own and embrace those qualities because they do, indeed, exist within me. I have been all of those things at various times in my life. And even though I strive not to be, there's always a chance I can and will be all those things again.

Contrary to how it might seem, I am not trying to denigrate, put myself down, or shame myself with these admissions. Nor do I use shadow work as an excuse to be those things.

The act of claiming and bringing these aspects of myself out into the light has been incredibly freeing. I feel lighter, brighter, and relieved.

The emotions, characteristics, aspects, and impulses you fear the most and try to hide usually hold the key to what is lacking in your life.

I am a selfish, controlling hypocrite. Oh, and a lazy, spoiled, know-it-all. Not to mention, I can be quite petty, small-minded, and mean. And a pathetic liar.

I am also generous, easy-going, and sincere. Oh, and active, grateful, and humble. Not to mention I can be quite receptive, open-minded, and kind. And a truth-teller.

> "When we suppress a feeling or impulse, we are also suppressing its polar opposite. If we deny our ugliness, we lessen our beauty. If we deny our fear, we minimize our courage. If we deny our greed, we also reduce our generosity... If you think someone is selfish, you can be sure that you are capable of demonstrating the same amount of selfishness. Although these qualities will not be expressed all the time, we each have the ability to act out any quality we see."
>
> —Debbie Ford, in *The Dark Side of the Light Chasers*

Humans judge. Judgment serves us. Except when it doesn't. Simply notice who, what, when, how, and why you judge. Don't judge yourself for being human. Be curious.

What do you judge her for?

_____

_____

_____

_____

_____

What does judging her do for you?

_____

_____

_____

_____

_____

What would it be like to stop judging her?

_____

_____

_____

_____

Do you want to?

_____

_____

_____

_____

Why or why not?

_____

_____

_____

SEPARATE

Separate (verb): to make a distinction between

> "Until you know who you are, separate from her, healthy
> boundaries will be nearly impossible."
>
> —Karen C.L. Anderson

One of the main causes of difficulty in mother-daughter relationships is a lack of differentiation or autonomy. It goes both ways. A mother may believe her daughter is her mini-me, just like her in all ways. A daughter may believe her mother lives and breathes simply because she (the daughter) exists.

You don't know where your thoughts and emotions start and hers end.

She believes in order for her to be happy, you have to think, feel, and act a certain way (so you don't know what you really think and feel or how you want to be).

You believe the same thing: in order to be happy, she has to think, feel, and act a certain way.

She tends to think she knows how you feel based on how she feels.

You have a tendency to think you know how she feels based on how you feel.

In order to have a healthy relationship based on mutual respect, it's helpful to emotionally separate and remember who you are. Sometimes, the separation needs to be physical in order to gain perspective (this is different than estrangement or going without contact).

The only person you need to take emotional responsibility for is yourself. You cannot make her happy, and she cannot make you happy.

When you focus on YOU—on your values, desires, needs, and preferences— something magical happens: the way you show up in your relationship with her (whether you choose to see or speak to her or not) changes in a way you never imagined possible.

You no longer tolerate abuse or engage in dysfunctional behavior.

You trust yourself to have and hold your boundaries not from a defensive, reactive place but from a solid, grounded place.

And there's nothing more respectful—to both of you—than that.

Where most of us get caught up is believing words like "separate" and "connected" are emotions. These words do not actually express emotion, they describe thoughts, opinions, and interpretations, which, when you think them, create emotion. They express how you interpret others, rather than how you feel. It's your interpretation that creates the emotion.

This is a crucially important distinction, because if you use words like these to describe emotion, you will inevitably experience powerlessness.

True connection is somewhat a paradox. It's possible when you and she are individual, autonomous women with your own thoughts, emotions, dreams, and desires. When you know, love, and trust yourself and she knows, loves, and trusts herself. When you can establish loving boundaries based on what you know, love, and trust about yourself, and when she is able to do the same. When the two of you let each other be who you are—the good, the bad, and the ugly.

The good news is she doesn't have to participate. She doesn't have to know, love, and trust herself the way you do or the way you think she should. The more connected you become to yourself, the more you can be open to connecting with her, no matter where she is on her journey.

Emotional separation is the solution and the medicine, not the thing that needs to be fixed or healed. You don't need to "make peace" with it because it IS peace.

What beliefs, values, and lessons did your mother teach directly (by telling you) and indirectly (via modeling)? Include beliefs about your body, food, sexuality, men, other women, people who are different than you, marriage, money, friendship, etc. Include things you're glad you learned and those you wish you hadn't.

_____

_____

_____

_____

_____

_____

_____

_____

_____

_____

What were her opinions about her body? Her friends? Food? Her marriage(s)? Her work inside the home? Her work outside the home if she had it?

_____

_____

_____

_____

_____

_____

_____

_____

_____

_____

_____

_____

_____

_____

_____

What do you believe?

_____

_____

_____

_____

Are these similar to what they taught?

_____

_____

_____

_____

What do you want to believe?

_____

_____

_____

_____

_____

Who are you, separate from her?

_____

_____

_____

_____

_____

Limit

Limit (noun): the utmost extent

> "Boundaries are the beautiful definition of who you are.
> They become instructions for people to get the best
> version of you."
>
> —Randi Buckley

What was your experience with boundaries when you were a child?

_____

_____

_____

_____

_____

What is your current experience with boundaries?

_____

_____

_____

_____

What would you like your experience with boundaries to be now?

_____

_____

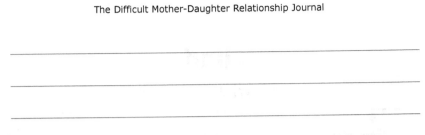

We often think of boundaries as defensive…about what we want to keep out. While that is true, the opposite is also true: boundaries are about what you value and what you want more of in your life.

They are simply (but not always easily) the act of creating space in your life for you to be the person you want to be (not who she thinks you should be). As such, healthy boundaries help you like, trust, and respect yourself more.

Why aren't they easy? Because you were most likely brought up in an authoritarian family culture that didn't promote autonomy. And while this dominating style of parenting "worked" in some ways, it also left you, as an adult, not sure of what you value. This, in turn, can make it hard for you set boundaries and even harder to enforce them.

What do you value? Make a list. If you're stuck, here's a brief list of values (you can also turn to Google and find all kinds of lists).

Abundance	Community	Equality
Acceptance	Competence	Equanimity
Accomplishment	Competition	Excellent
Accountability	Connection	Expansiveness
Achievement	Contentment	Exuberance
Accuracy	Contribution	Fairness
Adventure	Cooperation	Faithfulness
Affluence	Coordination	Flair
Aliveness	Courage	Freedom
Authenticity	Creativity	Friendship
Authority	Decisiveness	Fulfillment
Autonomy	Delight	Fun
Beauty	Determination	Generosity
Belonging	Desire	Goodwill
Bliss	Devotion	Goodness
Boldness	Discernment	Gratitude
Bravery	Discipline	Growth
Brazenness	Discovery	Happiness
Brilliance	Diversity	Hard work
Calm	Ease	Harmony
Centered	Efficiency	Health
Change	Elation	Honesty
Clarity	Empathy	Honor
Cleanliness	Empowerment	Humor
Collaboration	Encouragement	Imagination
Commitment	Energy	Impact
Communication	Enlightenment	Improvement

Independence	Performance	Sensitivity
Individuality	Personal growth	Service
Inner peace	Play	Simplicity
Innovation	Pleasure	Skill
Inspiration	Poise	Sovereignty
Integrity	Power	Speed
Intellect	Possibility	Spirituality
Intensity	Practicality	Stability
Joy	Presence	Status
Jubilation	Preservation	Strength
Justice	Privacy	Success
Kindness	Progress	Systemization
Knowledge	Prosperity	Tradition
Leadership	Purpose	Transparency
Love	Quality	Tranquility
Loyalty	Quiet	Trust
Luxury	Radiance	Truth
Magic	Relatedness	Unity
Mastery	Reliability	Value
Meaning	Resourcefulness	Vibrancy
Merit	Respect	Vitality
Nourishment	Responsibility	Wisdom
Openness	Responsiveness	Wonder
Optimism	Safety	Youthfulness
Passion	Satisfaction	
Peace	Security	
Perfection	Self-reliance	

Choose three to five values that sing to you…the values you want to grow and thrive in your life and in your relationship, with or without her.

How will you know which ones to choose? As you read and consider each value, notice when you feel a little zing or intake of breath that makes you sit up and take notice.

List them here, and write about why these specific values are important to you.

_____

_____

_____

_____

_____

_____

_____

_____

_____

_____

_____

_____

_____

_____

_____

_____

_____

_____

_____

_____

_____

_____

_____

_____

_____

_____

_____

_____

_____

_____

_____

These next writing prompts come from Randi Buckley's Healthy Boundaries for Kind People program (of which I am a certified facilitator).

_____

_____

_____

_____

_____

Thinking about the boundaries you wish to have, and ask yourself these questions, inserting your top values by turn in the blank space.

_____

_____

_____

_____

_____

"What would _____ do?"

_____

_____

_____

_____

"How can I bring _____ into situations that involve her?"

_____

_____

_____

_____

"When I feel or embody _____, my behavior reflects it.
I _____."

_____

_____

_____

_____

_____

"What would _____ do on my behalf?"

_____

_____

_____

_____

"If I was _____ representative in this situation, what would I do?"

_____

_____

_____

_____

"An example of a time I was fully living into _____ was…"

_____

_____

_____

_____

_____

∽

What does it feel like when you are living into these values?

_____

_____

_____

_____

_____

What takes you out of living these values?

_____

_____

_____

_____

Who is someone who knows your values and supports you in living them?

_____

_____

_____

_____

_____

How can you bring your values to life and into your surroundings as a reminder?

Paint them?

Dance them?

Write them?

Create an altar to them?

Vision board them?

Buy a piece of jewelry?

A crystal?

_____

_____

_____

_____

_____

_____

_____

_____

_____

_____

_____

_____

Or, try this:

Imagine you can create a semi-permeable bubble around you and fill it with whatever you like: kindness, creativity, respect, grace, humor, etc. Now, imagine feeling those traits/values/emotions around you. Remember the bubble is semipermeable. Some things can come in, and others can't. Only the things that can match the energy of what you are holding in your bubble can make it through. Other things will have to gently bounce off and can't get near you. Play with this. Monitor your bubble. Notice. Make choices. YOU choose what makes it through.

Make any additional notes here about ways you can put your values into action.

The Anatomy of a Healthy Boundary

The Request: ask her to stop doing whatever it is that crosses your boundary (you don't always have to say the request out loud, but it's important to be clear about it).

The Action: let her know *what you will do* if she chooses not to. It is an action that you will take. The more well-defined the action, the better and more effective your boundary will be.

The Benefit: be clear about the benefit this boundary will have in the relationship.

Here are some examples:

Request: Please stop yelling at me.

Action: If you continue to yell, I am going to leave.

Benefit: If you stop yelling, I'll be able to better concentrate on what you're trying to tell me.

Request: The best way to reach me is via email.

Action: If you text me or send me messages on Facebook, I won't respond.

Benefit: If you email, it's easier for me to keep track of our communication.

Request: I'd love to chat with you once a week for half an hour.

Action: If you call me more than that, I won't answer the phone.

Benefit: This way, I'll be able to give you my undivided attention.

Request + Action + Benefit = Healthy Boundary

> "Clear is kind. Unclear is unkind."
>
> —Brené Brown

Pick one boundary would you like to set with her.

_____

_____

_____

_____

Why this boundary?

_____

_____

_____

_____

What do you hope to accomplish with this boundary?

_____

_____

_____

_____

_____

What value can you put into action in support of this boundary?

_____

_____

_____

_____

_____

What does taking care of yourself look like?

_____

_____

_____

_____

What do you need to take responsibility for?

_____

_____

_____

_____

_____

What are your fears around having boundaries with her?

_____

_____

_____

_____

_____

Is there anything you're unwilling to think, feel, or do in order to have healthy boundaries? What are they?

_____

_____

_____

_____

_____

What are the costs of not setting a boundary with her?

_____

_____

_____

_____

_____

What's possible for you as a result of establishing and living with this boundary?

_____

_____

_____

_____

_____

Write your boundary using the request-action-benefit model. Say it to yourself. Say it out loud. Say it out loud while looking at yourself in the mirror. Say it out loud to someone else (not her), and see how it lands.

_____

_____

_____

_____

_____

_____

_____

_____

_____

How does it feel to say it out loud?

_____

_____

_____

_____

_____

When you imagine saying it to her, how do you feel?

_____

_____

_____

_____

_____

What action are you willing to take in support of your boundary?

_____

_____

_____

_____

_____

What is the benefit to you and/or your relationship with her?

_____

_____

_____

_____

_____

Are there other ways to communicate the boundary without words?

_____

_____

_____

_____

_____

Equally important as being able to communicate clear and healthy boundaries is the ability to receive and respond to the boundaries she wishes to have with you.

Remember, when you set a boundary, she doesn't have to respect it. Similarly, you don't have to respect her boundaries. If you choose not to, you can skip this section.

When she comes to you with a boundary, listen, acknowledge, and determine what action you can take that will honor her request. If she sets the boundary properly, she won't be counting on you to honor it...she will honor her own boundaries by changing her behavior.

What do you make it mean about you that she wants to set a boundary with you?

_____

_____

_____

_____

_____

How does it feel when she sets a boundary with you?

_____

_____

_____

_____

_____

_____

Do you want to honor/respect it? Why or why not?

_____

_____

_____

_____

_____

Do you want to thank her?

_____

_____

_____

_____

_____

Boundary-Setting Tips

1. Boundaries are not mean, rude, or selfish; disrespectful; orders; designed to control, manipulate, coerce, or threaten others; meant to change someone else's behavior; ultimatums; about the dynamics of a situation; weapons you deploy in anger; reactive.

2. Boundaries are healthy; respectful; about your behavior; a delineation of where you end and others start; a tool that promotes self-responsibility; a gift that creates both autonomy and connection; a meaningful way for you to take care of and protect yourself based on your values; about the decisions you want to make; responsive.

3. Decide you respect and value yourself enough to establish boundaries and that you respect and value her enough to teach her how to be with you.

4. Be clear about what you value, knowing your boundaries will be those values *in action* (thank you Randi Buckley for this distinction). When you are connected to your values in this way, your boundaries will feel like a more natural extension of who you are.

5. Be compassionate. You are modeling an important skill for effective communication. Being compassionate and setting boundaries go together.

6. If you're frustrated, angry, or resentful, work through those emotions first. Journal (or talk with someone who won't continue to validate your anger) until you can get to a space of calm. Revisit the somatic exercises on page 62. The reason you are upset is because you don't have proper boundaries in place, and you haven't been speaking your truth. Once you're clean and clear (which basically means you've taken responsibility for feeling upset), you can have a boundary conversation if you want to.

7. It's not necessary to communicate your boundaries until she has violated them. And even then, you don't necessarily have to communicate it, but in order to be effective, you do have to follow through with the action you promised yourself you would take.

8. If you choose to have a boundary conversation, use a neutral tone of voice. If there is a negative (or falsely positive) charge to your communication, then the message can get lost and the clarity of the boundary becomes clouded. Practice speaking without a charge in your voice so it feels natural.

9. Remember you are not trying to control her behavior. You are changing or adjusting your own behavior in response.

10. Practice your new skill with someone who will offer little resistance. Get a feel for what it is like to make the request. When you get more confident, you can start setting boundaries with her.

11. Be responsible for your own communication, but understand you are not responsible for how she receives or interprets it, nor for how she feels as a result. Create clear, direct ways of communicating and allow her to feel how she chooses.

12. Don't take it personally if she doesn't change or respect your boundary, and don't expect her to. Be ready, willing, and able to follow through a change in your own behavior.

Break

Break (noun): a pause

> "Relationships are eternal. The 'separation' is another chapter in the relationship. Often, letting go of the old form of the relationship becomes a lesson in pure love much deeper than any would have learned had you stayed together."
>
> —Marianne Williamson

(Williamson's quote is directed at romantic couples, but it applies here as well.)

There is no shame in taking time and space away from her in order to know and care for yourself. This is an excellent reason to suspend contact with her, and it doesn't have to be forever.

When you find yourself at the point of deciding whether to do it, it's agonizing on several levels: You don't want to have to make the decision, you're afraid of what will happen (either way), and you're afraid of what others will think.

You're stuck in the paralyzing and unsatisfying energy of "maybe"…of having not made a decision. It's not an easy or fun place to be: feeling that no matter what choice you make, it's the wrong choice.

You may think you have no other choice, but consider the choice isn't whether to go "no-contact" or not, the choice is in *how* you do it.

You can make the choice from a place of personal power and self-responsibility or you can make the choice from place of blame, reaction, or defensiveness.

Personal power and self-responsibility: *I can't manage or trust myself around her right now. It's hard for me to feel good around her, and I find myself wanting her to behave differently or change so I can feel better. And I am not going to beat myself up for not being able to trust myself yet.*

Blame, reaction, defensiveness: *She drives me crazy. She doesn't respect me, and I'm tired of feeling manipulated and taken advantage of. She has left me no choice—I'm done.*

If she's actively abusive, mean, violent, addicted, mentally ill, etc., taking a break is an act of kindness to yourself. Showing yourself kindness doesn't mean that you're unkind to her. Kindness never fails.

Ultimately, taking a break is about trusting yourself and focusing on what you want and need—right now. Women are generally not rewarded for doing that in our culture (in fact, they are often subtly punished), so there's a lot of fear and guilt associated with it.

No matter which path you choose, you don't have to tell yourself (and others) stories about how awful she is in order to take a break. If you want to tell stories about how awful she is, go for it. It can be cathartic to do so. But based on my own experience, it can keep you stuck and enmeshed with her when what you really want is freedom. When you trust yourself and your boundaries, you no longer have to tell stories that keep you stuck in a less-than position.

> "Whether or not I'm ever close to her again is not the issue.
> The issue is whether I accept that I am, that I've become,
> the type of person who doesn't have more than a cordial
> relationship with her."
>
> —A client

Why do you want to take a break from the relationship?

_____

_____

_____

_____

_____

Do you like and respect your reasons?

_____

_____

_____

_____

_____

What are your fears about taking a break?

_____

_____

_____

_____

Is it possible to do what you want to do and at the same time like and respect yourself through the process?

_____

_____

_____

_____

_____

_____

How would you like to approach taking a break?

_____

_____

_____

_____

What do you want to say to her?

_____

_____

_____

_____

Will you like and respect yourself if you do it that way?

_____

_____

_____

_____

How will you handle it if she tries to make contact with you?

_____

_____

_____

_____

_____

Need

Need (verb): require (something) because it is essential or very important

> "Neediness is SO beautiful. It's what allows our hearts to open. It's what brings us to our knees in surrender. It keeps us honest and real and oh-so-very tenderly human."
>
> —Chris Zydel

Humans have needs (and wants). And it's almost certain that she wasn't able to anticipate and meet all of your needs (and wants). It's also almost certain that each of you manipulated the other in order to get needs met.

In some ways, you were probably taught your wants and needs don't matter or your wants and needs are selfish or weak or annoying, etc. You may have resorted to unpleasant behaviors like manipulation in order to get your needs met. I know I have, and I know it's a pattern that shows up in my maternal lineage.

When I was a little girl spending time with my grandmother, she'd often say things like, "I'm tired, take a nap." Or, "I'm cold, put on a sweater."

Another way this kind of manipulation and control can show up is when you hear others say things like, "You're not hungry" or, "Stop being so dramatic."

Over time, you are no longer attuned to your own needs.

When you are aware of (and not judging yourself for) your needs and wants, your actions reflect it. Your actions also reflect when your needs and wants are not being met.

In this section, you get to explore your needs and wants as they relate to your relationship with her without judgment (as always).

What did you need from her that you did not get?

_____

_____

_____

_____

_____

What did you want?

_____

_____

_____

_____

_____

Where did she fall short?

_____

_____

_____

_____

What didn't you receive that you needed and/or wanted?

_____

_____

_____

_____

_____

What are the consistent, negative thoughts running through your mind about your needs and wants?

_____

_____

_____

_____

Are they your own thoughts, or are they her thoughts?

_____

_____

_____

_____

Can you start to acknowledge, honor, and meet your own needs and wants (or get them met in a healthy way)?

_____

_____

_____

_____

_____

In what areas of your life are you not kind and gentle with yourself?

_____

_____

_____

_____

_____

How can you demonstrate to yourself (and others, including your own children, if you have them) that you matter?

_____

_____

_____

_____

_____

Do you love yourself as you are, without needing to change?

_____

_____

_____

_____

_____

Where do you need to love yourself more?

_____

_____

_____

_____

_____

Can you love yourself and provide yourself with comfort even in the face of uncomfortable emotions?

_____

_____

_____

_____

_____

Write a letter to yourself from your future self, from where you want to be in your relationship with yourself and with her, and have your future self give you advice. What would she tell you to stop doing? To start doing? What does she tell you about what you need and want? What does your future self want you to do now, so you can like and respect yourself and your needs? Anything else?

_____

_____

_____

_____

_____

_____

Need

Heal

Heal (verb): to transform that which is a source of suffering into something that is a source of wisdom and liberation

> "Your wound is probably not your fault, but your healing is your responsibility."
>
> —Unknown

How can you remove suffering from your story about her?

_____

_____

_____

_____

What do you need to believe about yourself in order not to suffer?

_____

_____

_____

_____

What do you need to believe about her in order not to suffer?

_____

_____

What do you need to believe about your relationship with her in order not to suffer?

What wisdom do your emotions hold?

What wisdom does your story about her hold?

What wisdom does your story about your relationship with her hold?

_____

_____

_____

_____

_____

What does freedom and liberation look like when you think about your relationship with her?

_____

_____

_____

_____

_____

Reconnect (or Not)

Reconnect (verb): reestablish a bond of communication or emotion

If you are currently not in contact with her, you may have made that choice intending it to be forever.

You may have taken a break because you didn't know how to handle the dysfunction, codependence, and emotional enmeshment. You probably thought it was the only way to feel better.

You may now realize a more effective way to feel better is focusing on yourself: your thoughts, your emotions, your actions. You probably didn't want to do that at first because you were living both "in reaction" and "in resistance" to her.

You didn't trust yourself because you didn't know who you were apart from her.

Taking a break from your relationship with her can help you get to know yourself better. You find you respect and trust yourself more because you are grounded in your values and preferences.

You have told the truth.

Now you are here, you may (or may not) want to reinitiate contact.

∽

Why do you want to reinitiate contact?

_____

_____

_____

_____

_____

_____

What are your hopes for doing so?

_____

_____

_____

_____

_____

_____

Do you like and respect your reasons?

_____

_____

_____

_____

_____

_____

What boundaries do you need to have in place?

_____

_____

_____

_____

_____

_____

_____

Do you trust yourself to honor your boundaries?

_____

_____

_____

_____

_____

_____

_____

Revisit

Revisit (verb): to consider or take up again

It's time to revisit your intention.

What was your intention when you set out on this journey?

What did you discover?

What is different now?

What is the same?

What are you bringing with you into the future?

What are you leaving behind?

What is no longer true?

What is true?

Revisit

_____

_____

_____

_____

_____

_____

_____

_____

_____

_____

And so it is.

Practice

Practice (verb): apply an idea, belief, or method

We don't "get it" all at once and then go off and live a perfect life. We often have to "get it" many times in order to live it, and even then, it's never perfect (and that's okay).

That's why we practice. It's a way of ensuring a continual "getting."

Practice awareness.

Practice setting boundaries that serve you and strengthen the relationships that mean the most to you.

Practice taking good care of your physical, mental, spiritual, and emotional self.

Practice meeting your own needs and asking for help in doing so.

Practice showing up in the world on purpose, knowing it's always your choice to do so.

Practice feeling.

Practice having your own back.

Practice loving yourself.

Practice acknowledging loss.

Practice grieving well.

Practice giving yourself permission to choose any and all emotions.

Practice not judging your thoughts and emotions as good or bad, right or wrong.

Practice acceptance.

And now? Imagine the positive impact of your practice on future generations. The women in your maternal lineage may not have been able to model what you needed them to, but there's no reason you can't stretch now.

Write a letter to future generations describing the journey you've chosen to take, the story you now stand on, and your hopes and dreams for them.

_____

_____

_____

_____

_____

_____

_____

_____

_____

_____

_____

_____

_____

_____

Practice

Recommended Reading & Other Resources

The Atlas of Emotions (http://atlasofemotions.org)

Bradford, Dr. Joy Harden: founder of Therapy for Black Girls (http://www.therapyforblackgirls.com)

Buckley, Randi: creator of Healthy Boundaries for Kind People (http://randibuckley.com)

The Center for Self Leadership/Internal Family Systems (http://www.selfleadership.org/)

Coleman, Dr. Joshua: author of *When Parents Hurt: Compassionate Strategies When You And Your Grown Child Don't Get Along* (http://www.drjoshuacoleman.com/)

Cunningham, Jane: (http://numinousjane.com) writer and creator of Facing the Minotaur

EMDR Institute (http://www.emdr.com/)

Ferraro, Kris: author of *Energy Healing: Simple & Effective Practices to Become Your Own Healer* (http://www.krisferraro.com)

Ford, Debbie: author of *The Dark Side of the Light Chasers* (http://debbieford.com)

Forrest, Lynne: author of *Beyond Victim Consciousness* (http://lynneforrest.com)

Forward, Dr. Susan: author of *Mothers Who Can't Love: A Healing Guide for Daughters* (http://www.susanforward.com/)

Gibson, Dr. Lindsay: author of *Adult Children of Emotionally Immature Parents* (http://www.drlindsaygibson.com/)

Helander, Ingrid: therapist/coach specializing in Internal Family Systems (http://ingridyhelanderlmft.com/)

Inge, Christie: master energy healer, confidence coach, and creator of Shadow & Light and WonderWork (http://christieinge.com)

Johnson, Kimberly: Somatic Experiencing practitioner, author, and creator of Activate Your Inner Jaguar (http://www.magamama.com/)

Mártir, Vanessa: writer and creator of Writing Our Lives Workshops (http://www.vanessamartir.com/)

Maté, Dr. Gabor: trauma specialist and author (http://drgabormate.com)

McBride, Dr. Karyl: author of *Will I Ever Be Good Enough* (http://www.willieverbegoodenough.com/)

McLaren, Karla: author of *The Language of Emotions* (http://karlamclaren.com)

Northrup, Dr. Christiane: author of *Mother-Daughter Wisdom* (http://drnorthrup.com)

Porges, Dr. Stephen: "father" of polyvagal theory and expert in the evolution of the human nervous system (http://stephenporges.com/)

Schwartz, Dr. Arielle: author of *The Complex PTSD Workbook: A Mind-Body Approach to Regaining Emotional Control & Becoming Whole* (http://drarielleschwartz.com/)

Shelton, Staci Jordan: performance consultant and coach who specializes in dealing barriers to performance beyond process (http://stacijordanshelton.com)

The Somatic Experiencing Trauma Institute (http://traumahealing.org/)

TRE for All (http://traumaprevention.com)

Tsabary, Dr. Shefali: author of *The Conscious Parent* and *The Awakened Family* (http://drshefali.com)

Turner, Toko-pa: author of *Belonging: Remembering Ourselves Home* (http://toko-pa.com/)

Walker, Rebecca: author of Baby Love: *Choosing Motherhood After a Lifetime of Ambivalence* (http://www.rebeccawalker.com)

Webster, Bethany: writer and creator of Womb of Light (http://womboflight.com)

West, Lena: founder of CEO DNA and Business Coach for Womxn Entrepreneurs (http://lenawest.com)

Wolynn, Mark: author of *It Didn't Start With You* (http://www.markwolynn.com/)

Acknowledgments

Gratitude (I am literally feeling it as I write this) to the team at Mango, especially my editor, Brenda Knight; to my agent Kristen Moeller, who saw the potential before I did and continues to hold the vision; to my friend and partner in AFGOs Christie Inge; to Tanya Geisler, who always reminds me of what I want and mentors me through my Impostor Complex; to Brenda, Nancy, Julie, Sally, and Kristen, who read and re-read my words and cheer me on ceaselessly; to Karen G., who reached out on that fateful Christmas Day; to my stepdaughter Jessica Carlson who, without knowing it, held the mirror up and had me doing some of the best and deepest work of my life; and finally to my husband and partner in life Tim Anderson, who sees the whole me and loves the whole me and who created a safe place for me to reveal and heal my own patterns.

About the Author

Karen C.L. Anderson is the international best-selling author of *Difficult Mothers, Adult Daughters: A Guide for Separation, Liberation & Inspiration.* She works with women on revealing and healing their difficult mother-daughter relationship stories and is writing a memoir, *A Letter to the Daughter I Chose Not to Have.*

She lives in Southeastern Connecticut.

Thank You

Stay in touch by signing up for my weekly Love Notes (answers to your questions, advice, essays, excerpts from books, offers, and other bits of wisdom delivered to your inbox every Thursday): www.kclanderson.com/subscribe.

If you are interested in having my guidance as you work through this journal, please send me an email: karen@kclanderson.com. I offer 1:1 coaching to mothers and daughters (separately or together).

Contact information:

Phone: 760-632-9190
Email: admin@waterside.com
Website: http://kclanderson.com
Facebook: http://facebook.com/KarenCLAnderson/
Instagram: KCLAnderson

Agent:

Waterside Productions Inc.
2055 Oxford Avenue
Cardiff by the Sea, CA 92007

Mango Publishing, established in 2014, publishes an eclectic list of books by diverse authors — both new and established voices — on topics ranging from business, personal growth, women's empowerment, LGBTQ studies, health, and spirituality to history, popular culture, time management, decluttering, lifestyle, mental wellness, aging, and sustainable living. We were recently named 2019's #1 fastest growing independent publisher by *Publishers Weekly*. Our success is driven by our main goal, which is to publish high quality books that will entertain readers as well as make a positive difference in their lives.

Our readers are our most important resource; we value your input, suggestions, and ideas. We'd love to hear from you — after all, we are publishing books for you!

Please stay in touch with us and follow us at:

Facebook: Mango Publishing
Twitter: @MangoPublishing
Instagram: @MangoPublishing
LinkedIn: Mango Publishing
Pinterest: Mango Publishing

Sign up for our newsletter at www.mango.bz and receive a free book!

Join us on Mango's journey to reinvent publishing, one book at a time.

CPSIA information can be obtained
at www.ICGtesting.com
Printed in the USA
BVHW072048300920
590031BV00004B/7